A Programmer's Guide to Personal Finance

William M. Springer II

Jaxson Media

Contents

Chapter One

Introduction

There are many books on retirement and other financial topics. Why one specifically for programmers?

Programmers are somewhat unique, financially, in that we both tend to be fairly well paid and have an above average ability to start our own businesses or side hustles that can cover our expenses. As such, our financial considerations may be a bit different from those of people without the same income producing ability (most of the population) or whose income is tied more directly to particular ways of earning money (e.g., medical doctors).

In this book, I'll cover the usual things that everyone needs to know (taxes and social security), but with an emphasis on things that are particularly likely to be relevant to small business owners and those with a significant amount of disposable income.

While much of this book applies no matter where you live, parts are specifically about the law in the United States. If you're not an American and do not live in the US, those parts probably don't apply to you. ***Also, I am not a tax professional, a lawyer, or an accountant, just someone who enjoys finance, has started multiple successful businesses, and***

has run an investment group for a number of years. No guarantees are made or implied.

Chapter Two

Debt and Spending

When it comes to debt, many people fall into one of two extremes. At one end, you have people who use debt for everything, whenever they want something that they don't have the money for, and quickly end up with maxed out credit cards and no idea how they can dig themselves out of the hole. At the other end you have people who refuse to use debt at all, only buying what they can pay for in cash.

The healthy behavior is to recognize that there is good debt and bad debt and avoid the bad debt. Good debt helps you to reach your financial goals; bad debt does not.

For me, I have used debt to start two businesses, purchase two homes, and earn a PhD. Income-generating businesses, real estate, and education are assets – things that can be used to improve your financial position. This is good debt.

I have also used debt for impulse purchases. This is bad debt – you end up still paying for things long after those things have reached the end of their usefulness.

Many would-be gurus in the personal finance area will tell you to give up small purchases because they add up over time. A $6 coffee each workday, for example, adds up to $45,000 over the course of a 30-year career. That sounds like a lot – and it is! On the other hand, someone making a $100k salary will earn $3 million over that same time period, and may very well be happier during it due to his expensive coffee.

The real problems to deal with are impulse spending and lifestyle inflation. As your income increases, it's common that your spending increases to keep pace. Maybe you were previously happy with one or two visits to Starbucks each week and a Camry, but now want daily Starbucks and a Model S. As a result, it's difficult to save a larger percentage of your salary despite earning more, because your daily living expenses keep growing along with your income.

This is where budgeting can be helpful. "Budget" is one of those words that often makes people groan (myself included). The key is to realize that the point is not to avoid spending money, but to ensure you're spending money on the things you want to spend it on rather than on impulse purchases. It's fine to buy whatever you want, as long as you're tracking where the money is going and not spending more than you really wanted to.

The key is to splurge on things that make you happy and save on things that don't. I recently spent over a thousand dollars on professional photos, which some people would consider extravagant but we know we'll enjoy for years. I moved to a house closer to work so I would have a shorter commute. These are expenses that result in an improvement to my quality of life. Invest in things that improve your quality of life; skimp on the things that don't.

Chapter Three

Time and money

We spend our time to make money. We use money to buy back time. The trick is to do both efficiently.

I believe in investing money in things that will improve your life in a noticeable way, such as by improving your health, removing a noticeable annoyance, or just saving money in the long run.

Examples of health-related spending could be a standing desk and a good ergonomic keyboard and mouse. These help you avoid health problems in the long run. Removing an annoyance could mean living closer to work (less time and gas wasted on a commute) or hiring someone to clean your gutters rather than doing it yourself. If you have a good side hustle, it's quite possible that the extra time spent working on that is worth more than the money you would pay to have someone else do a task you don't want to do.

Paying for quality often means that your possessions last longer (in addition to being nicer). I'm still using the cookware I bought in 2004 (although I have more of it now), and I expect our nice wood dining table to last indefinitely. If you need a tool one time, find a cheap one; if you want something to last, expect to pay more.

Most relevantly for your income, purchase tools that help you to make better use of your time. If an extra monitor or curved ultrawide monitor makes you more efficient, it will quickly pay for itself. Consider – if you value your time at $50/hour and a $500 tool makes you only 5% more efficient, it will pay for itself in 200 hours of use. How many hours per year do you spend in front of your computer?

On the other hand, avoid spending money on things that don't accomplish one of those goals. As mentioned above, lifestyle inflation is a very real thing; spending tends to increase along with income, so it's hard to get ahead. How many of the things you've spent money on in the last year made a noticeable difference in your life?

Chapter Four

Stock Market Investing

"In the short run, the market is a voting machine but in the long run, it is a weighing machine."

—— Benjamin Graham

As a rule, software developers are smart people who are good at analyzing things. This can be dangerous when it comes to investing, because we have a tendency to look at the stock market and see a system that we can analyze. There are two problems with this.

The first is that the stock market does not always behave rationally. At any given time, the price of a stock represents the consensus value of the underlying company, which may or may not reflect its actual value. Making money by buying and selling individual stocks requires figuring out which way the market will move, which is extremely difficult; almost no professional investors are able to consistently beat the market.

The second is that you're competing against people who do nothing except play the market, but have access to way more money, information, and execution speed[1] than you do.

That said, it's certainly possible – even easy – to make money investing in the stock market. When you purchase a stock, you are buying partial ownership in a company. As the economy grows over time, the total value of the stock market (which represents the portion of the economy made up of publicly traded companies) rises as well.

However, this says nothing about the behavior of individual stocks – any given company can certainly go bankrupt, leaving the stock worthless. Thus, the safest and easiest way for most people to invest is simply to buy the entire market.

Interacting with the stock market

The US stock market alone contains thousands of different stocks valued at tens of trillions of dollars. Rather than purchasing individual stocks, most people buy multiple stocks that have been bundled in various ways.

A mutual fund is an actively-managed investment vehicle, which means that investors pool their funds and someone (a fund manager) makes decisions about what to purchase. These funds charge a fee, generally a percentage of your balance, to cover the manager's services. Funds may invest primarily in stocks, bonds, or a combination.

Exchange Traded Funds (ETFs) are similar to mutual funds, but are treated like stocks in that they can be sold short (selling something you don't have), purchased on margin (that is, with borrowed money), or optioned (purchasing or selling the right to buy or sell the ETF).

---

1. For more on this, look up High Frequency Trading.

Index funds are funds that are not actively managed, but instead simply buy a market index, such as the S&P 500. As a result, the expenses for owning such a fund tend to be very low. By purchasing a fund which tracks the entire market, you can get essentially the same return as the stock market with no additional work, and most people would benefit from choosing this option.

A balanced fund uses asset allocation, which we will discuss below, in order to increase returns. Asset allocation is a way to ensure that we don't have too much exposure to any particular segment of the market.

Asset allocation

Often, different sectors of the stock market will be moving in different directions. While the market as a whole might be going up, down, or sideways, certain types of assets may behave differently. Traditionally, this means having a mix of stocks and bonds (and cash). Even though stocks generally offer a higher rate of return than bonds, having both can actually increase the expected growth of your portfolio. What you will do is decide what percentage of your portfolio you want each type of asset to be, invest accordingly, and occasionally rebalance to bring your portfolio back to the desired allocation.

For example, suppose you choose an 80/20 ratio of stocks to bonds. You set up your investments to go 80% into stocks, 20% into bonds. After a year, stocks have gone up more than bonds, so you sell some stock and purchase bonds. After another year, stocks have fallen, so you sell bonds to purchase stocks. In this way, you lock in gains from the type of asset that is doing well, while purchasing the other type of asset while it is on sale.

We can extend this to various sectors of the stock market – healthcare, energy, technology, real estate, and so on. If I want to invest in technology and healthcare, I can purchase a mutual fund or ETF that specializes in each of those sectors, then occasionally sell one and buy the other to keep the two equally weighted in my portfolio.

Other ways to choose stocks

Aside from buying the entire market or sectors of it, investors often pursue a particular kind of earnings. Growth investors look for companies they think will outperform the market over time due to their future potential. Value investors look for stocks that they think are priced below their real value. Dividend investors look for companies with a history of paying a strong dividend[2], which they can continue to collect regardless of whether the stock price goes up or down.

2. A company that pays dividends returns some of its profits to its shareholders, rather than re-investing it in the business or buying back its own shares. Many people like to invest in dividend aristocrats, which have paid increasing dividends for at least 25 years running, or dividend kings, which have done the same for at least 50 years.

Chapter Five

Taxes

"Nothing is certain except death and taxes" – Benjamin Franklin

"The difference between death and taxes is death doesn't get worse every time Congress meets" – Will Rogers

Ask the average person what the purpose of taxes is, and you'll likely hear something about funding the government. At the state and local level, this is true. At the federal level, this is not entirely true; because the United States uses fiat currency, money is actually created by government spending. Rather, taxes serve three purposes:

1. They help to regulate the money supply. Removing money from circulation limits inflation, and requiring that taxes be paid in US dollars creates demand for those dollars, allowing the government to use them for purchases.

2. They help keep money circulating through the economy.

3. They influence behavior (in the form of tax breaks for things the government wants to encourage).

This isn't an economics textbook, so we'll say no more about this; just realize there are reasons that the tax code is the way it is. Understanding how it works helps you to put yourself in the best financial position.

Marginal tax rates

When your income increases to the point where you find yourself in a new tax bracket, only your income over the threshold is subject to the new tax rate.

Suppose that $89,451 is the start of the 22% tax bracket (which is true as of 2023, for a married couple) and you're making $1 less than that. You now get a $5000 raise. Only that $5000 is taxed at the new rate; the rest of your income is taxed the same way it was before.

The clear implication of this is that increasing your income is always a net gain, so far as income tax brackets go. It is possible to take home less money after an increase in income, but this would happen only in the very specific situation that you are no longer eligible for a tax credit you previously took and which was worth more than the additional money you're making. For example, the electric vehicle tax credit, as of 2023, has an income cap of $150k for individuals or $300k for couples. If your income increased from $1 under the limit to $1 over for the year you purchased a qualifying electric vehicle, you would lose the $7500 credit! For the most part, however, this type of credit is targeted at lower income individuals; while it's possible that you qualify for them now, our goal is to increase your income sufficiently that they'll soon cease to be a consideration.

FICA

For most people, one of the biggest paycheck deductions is FICA, which funds Medicare and Social Security, each of which is funded by this dedicated income stream rather than out of general revenues[1]. As an employee, you pay 6.2% of your salary towards Social Security and an additional 1.45% towards Medicare. Your employer pays the same amount; if you are self-employed, you pay both sides[2].

Social Security is longevity insurance; it's not intended on its own to provide a comfortable retirement, but to keep you from starving if you outlive your money. As such, the Social Security trust fund ($2.805 trillion as of 2022) is held in the safest investment possible: US treasuries. Think of it as a lifetime annuity: the return isn't great, but it pays out indefinitely. It pays you enough to survive on, while your investments (hopefully) pay enough to live on. Depending on your income in retirement, Social Security benefits may or may not be taxable; we'll cover that when we discuss how much money you'll need to retire. You pay Social Security tax on (as of 2023) the first $160,200 of your earned income; income over the cap and unearned income (such as dividends and capital gains) are not subject to the tax.

Medicare provides healthcare for people over 65. Despite this being (by far) the most expensive group to insure, economies of scale and millions of

---

1. Yes, I said that taxes don't fund government spending, but we pretend they do. If nothing else, keeping revenue reasonably close to spending helps regulate the money supply.

2. There is an additional 3.8% surcharge on investment income for couples with an AGI (adjusted gross income) over $250k (or an individual with AGI over $200k).

younger people paying into the system keeps rates reasonable[3]. Everyone should generally sign up for Medicare when they turn 65, although you don't have to start using it right away if you have private insurance through work.

If you're under the age of 62, you probably don't have to think about these programs much, except when planning healthcare expenses in retirement. Just be aware of self-employment tax (what we call it when you pay the employer portion of FICA as well as your own portion) if you decide to work for yourself.

Unearned income

Unearned income (income not from a job) is treated differently. It is not subject to FICA and often receives preferential tax treatment.

For example, when you buy and then sell a stock, the price difference is a capital gain (or loss). If you held the stock for less than a year, this is a short term capital gain and is taxed as ordinary income. When you hold it for more than a year, this is a long term capital gain and is taxed at 0%, 15%, or 20%.

Similarly, ordinary dividends are taxed as ordinary income, but qualified dividends are taxed at the long term capital gains rate. Dividends were discussed in the stock market chapter.

---

3. Medicare part A, which covers hospital services, generally has no premium. In 2023, monthly Medicare premiums range from $164.90 to $560.50, depending on income; a couple with AGI no more than $194k will pay the lowest amount. Part D, which provides drug coverage, has a monthly premium ranging from $0 to $76.40 depending on income.

Alternative Minimum Tax (AMT)

The AMT helps ensure fairness in the tax code by effectively setting a minimum tax rate for high-income taxpayers; it does this by disallowing certain deductions. Someone subject to the AMT pays a tax rate of 26% on taxable income under $206,100 and 28% on income over that limit, if this would be greater than the amount of taxes as normally calculated. This is instead of, rather than in addition to, their normal tax rate. This incentivizes increasing your income over seeking tax shelters.

Real estate taxes and tax credits

Real estate is interesting, from a tax perspective, because you will (in most states) pay taxes on your home while also having the option of taking a tax credit.

For historical reasons, schools are usually funded out of property taxes, which are assessed as a percentage of the property's value. At the same time, the federal tax code was written to benefit property owners, and there are multiple provisions of the tax code that encourage the purchase of real estate. Some are meant to encourage homeownership, while others apply to rental property.

From a homeowner's perspective, the two most relevant provisions are the SALT deduction and the primary home tax exclusion. SALT is short for State and Local Taxes; it allows you to deduct the amount you pay in city and state taxes (including property tax and your choice of either income tax or sales tax) from your income for federal tax purposes[4]. However, the 2017 tax law changes capped this deduction at $10k. This cap, combined with other changes, makes taking the standard deduction more attractive for most people[5].

The primary home exemption allows you to exclude $250k ($500k for couples) in appreciation from the sale of your primary home (that is, the main home you've owned and lived in for at least two of the previous five years). For example, suppose you purchased a home for $220k, spent $20k renovating it, and took $30k in deductions over the time you owned it. Your basis (how much you have invested in the property) is 220+20-30=$210k. If you now sell the house for $400k, you have a profit of $190k, which is less than the exclusion, so you don't owe any taxes on the gains. The renovation was an example of a capital improvement, which is something that adds value to the home: while you don't get an immediate

---

4. If you use tax preparation software, this is why it will ask you how much you paid in property taxes. It will also deduct either an estimate of how much sales tax you paid or the state income tax you paid, whichever is greater. However, if you made large purchases and kept close track of how much sales tax you paid, you can use the actual amount rather than the average amount.

5. A tax deduction reduces the amount of income you have to pay taxes on. A tax credit reduces the amount of tax you have to pay. Therefore, a credit is almost always better than a deduction. Taxpayers can either take the standard deduction (which is a flat amount per person) or itemize (in which case they add up individual deductions). Tax software will calculate your return both ways and take whichever gives you more money. Since credits are applied to reduce the amount of taxes due (or increase your refund), they can be used regardless of which deduction method you choose.

tax benefit from capital improvements, they increase the effective cost of the home and reduce the amount of money that may be subject to taxation when you sell[6].

There are also tax credits available for making energy-efficient improvements to your home. For example, the 2022 Inflation Reduction Act increased the credit for installing solar panels to 30% of the cost, which can make them extremely profitable to install[7]. There are credits for installing energy-efficient appliances and better windows and doors as well.

Be aware that unless it is done as part of a renovation, standard repairs (such as fixing a broken window or repainting a wall) are generally not deductible.

Retirement plans

Retirement plans allow you to invest your savings in a tax-advantaged way. These generally come in two types:

Traditional: A traditional account is funded with pretax dollars; that is, money you have not yet paid income tax on. The money is taxed when you withdraw it. This means that the money you would normally have paid in

---

6. For examples of allowable improvements, see IRS publication 523 on selling your home at https://www.irs.gov/publications/p523#en_US_2020_publink100010755

7. I had solar panels installed on my house, with a 20-year loan at 0.49% interest. At that interest rate, I will pay back 105% of the cost of the panels. At the same time, I will get a 30% tax credit. Assuming a 7% annual return, after 20 years this will be worth 116% of the system cost – and this is before I even generate any electricity!

taxes instead earns additional money for years before Uncle Sam takes his cut.

Roth: A Roth account is funded with after-tax dollars – money you've already paid your income taxes on and can now keep. Where you would normally have to pay taxes on your earnings (as either ordinary income or long term capital gains, depending on how long you held your investment), Roth withdrawals of both contributions and earnings are tax free, which means that money you invest now can grow for decades without you ever having to pay any taxes on what you make. This makes Roth accounts a huge win for those who are young or are currently in a low tax bracket.

The two main retirement plans are a 401k and an IRA, both of which can be either traditional or Roth. A 401k is an employer-sponsored plan with a contribution limit of $22,500 per year. Additionally, employers offering a 401k will generally have a matching program, where they match 50% or more of the money you contribute to your plan, up to a certain percentage of your salary. This is free money that you get simply for saving you should be doing anyway, which means that maxing out the match should be your primary investment goal each year.

IRAs are not tied to your employer; you set one up yourself. They have lower contribution limits as well ($6500 per year or the amount of your earned income, whichever is lower). Unlike employer-based plans, which may offer a limited number of funds to invest in, IRAs generally give you access to the entire market[8]. They do have income limits after which Roth

---

8. A good 401k plan may offer a brokerage option, which allows you to invest in stocks, bonds, and mutual funds as you see fit.

IRAs are no longer available and contributions to traditional IRAs can no longer be deducted[9].

The disadvantage of retirement plans is that, because they are intended specifically to save for retirement, under most circumstances you cannot withdraw your contributions without paying both any deferred taxes and an additional fee. Roth IRAs are the exception – the contributions (but not earnings) can be withdrawn at any time, without penalty. IRAs also have some special options you can use for family members:

- A spousal IRA allows a working spouse to contribute to IRAs for both themselves and a non-working spouse. Each IRA is still in only one person's name.

- A custodial Roth IRA (or Roth IRA for minors) allows a child to have their own IRA. The minor must have earned income, which includes things like babysitting in addition to traditional jobs. Note that it's not required that the child's income be used to fund the IRA – you can do that – only that they have the income (and that it is documented, either by filing taxes or in some type of written log). In addition to saving for retirement, the funds can be used for college expenses without penalty (although taxes may still be due on any earnings withdrawn before age 59 ½).

One final benefit of Roth IRAs is that there is no required minimum distribution, which means your money can keep growing (untaxed) until your death, at which time your heirs can let it grow for an additional ten

9. However, there is a strategy called a backdoor Roth, where after-tax dollars are contributed to a traditional IRA and that IRA is then converted into a Roth.

years before they need to withdraw the money. Holders of traditional IRAs and 401(k) accounts must withdraw at least a certain amount every year after reaching age 72.

Chapter Six

Starting a business

The key to a successful business is resolving some type of pain point for your customers.

For a doctor, this may be actual pain. For a plumber, a leaky pipe. For Angry Birds, boredom. The key is that your potential customers don't actually care about the product or service you're offering; what they care about is whether you're going to make their lives better.

You don't have to be the only one addressing their pain; you just have to do it in a way that's better, faster, cheaper, or more convenient than the competition. For example, consider the area of word processing. Microsoft Word is the standard, but is also the most expensive. Google Docs is free, but requires an internet connection. Scrivener makes it easy to rearrange chapters and save extra information that shouldn't actually appear in the final document, but isn't as full-featured as the others. Each of these products is addressing the same problem (how to create a document) but with a slightly different focus, which makes each of them better for different use cases, and in fact the same person may use all three for different purposes.

First mover advantage is definitely a thing - if there's no good solution available for your customers' pain point, then your offering is the only alternative and you have no competition to deal with. On the other hand, if there's no competition, this may very well mean that people either aren't interested in your offering or aren't willing to pay for it. The first step to deciding on an offer is to make sure that it's something people (preferably people who don't know you) want and will pay for. When there's already competition, this may have already been done for you, as you can see that others are making a profit - but to join in, you'll need to be able to demonstrate that your offer is clearly better in some way (and sufficiently better that your customers will choose you over the better-known offerings).

When I started working on A Programmer's Guide to Computer Science, I was fairly sure there would be interest because I saw people at conferences who wanted to learn the kind of information I wanted to write about. I gave talks on this material and saw that people were interested (and I was actually asked if I had a book). When I started writing, I got confirmation from my beta readers that this was something they found useful and were willing to pay for. There wasn't really any competition, so I had to verify the market myself before I spent several years working on my book.

Recurring revenue

One reason that Software as a Service (SaaS) is popular is that it gives you recurring revenue: your customers keep paying you monthly, quarterly, or annually. It's generally more expensive to acquire a new customer than to keep the ones you already have, so signing people up for a subscription makes each sale more profitable, because you spend less to make each sale.

However, there are several other ways to increase your revenue per customer. One is by having an upsell: when a customer purchases one product, you also offer them another, more expensive product. For example, someone purchasing an ebook might be offered a discount on an online course; someone purchasing the course might be offered a discount on personal training or an ongoing mentorship. As the customer just spent money on your product, they're potentially open to purchasing a higher level product.

Of course, you don't have to be offering something more expensive; you can just improve the value of a customer by increasing the number of items purchased. At the grocery store, items that are used together are frequently stocked together (for example, chocolate syrup in the ice cream aisle); online shopping systems will suggest related items you might be interested in. Most authors try to publish regularly, on the assumption that someone who enjoys one book is likely to purchase additional books by the same author.

The interesting thing about having recurring revenue is that because the average lifetime value of a customer is greater than the amount earned from their first purchase, the product provider is often willing to accept a customer acquisition cost (the amount spent to earn the first sale) greater than the profit made on that sale.

For example, I subscribe to Kindle Unlimited (recurring revenue for Amazon). I recently read a book series where the author probably makes about $1.20 per read, and so far there are six books out. If there is a 60% readthrough from book 1 to book 2 and a 90% readthrough for the rest of the series, then someone who reads the first book will, on average, read 1 + 0.6 + 0.54 + 0.49 + 0.44 + 0.39 = 3.46 books in the series, earning the author a total of around $4.15[1]. As long as the customer acquisition cost is below $4.15, that customer will on average be profitable, even if the author takes a loss on the first book.

There are two key pieces to this model. First, you have to have a good product[2]. Customers who purchase one of your products (or do a one-month trial, etc.) and don't care for it aren't going to keep buying from you, so you've potentially lost money. Second, you need to know your average lifetime profit from each customer and be able to acquire customers for less than this amount[3].

---

1. An author actually doing this calculation would of course use the real amount for each book, which will vary due to length, and factor in purchases as well as borrows, but we're keeping things simple. Also, readthrough on later books in a series can often be closer to 95%. Some authors write dozens of books in a series, so one loyal fan can be very profitable in the long run.

2. This assumes the product is something people want, at a price they're willing to pay, as discussed above. The best product in the world won't sell if people don't want it.

3. Of course, it doesn't have to be exact. If your cost of customer acquisition is less than what you make on the first sale, then everything after that is profit. Knowing the lifetime value of a customer just tells you how much you can afford to spend on acquisition without losing money.

Chapter Seven

Employee compensation

When starting your own businesses, the first step is to calculate how much money you'll actually need to replace your income as an employee. One rough estimate is that you should plan to double your hourly pay! This is for three reasons.

1. If you're contracting and charging hourly or by project, you're no longer guaranteed to get paid for 40 hours per week.

2. You're now responsible for self-employment taxes, as described in the previous section.

3. You need to replace your benefits, which can make up a significant portion of your compensation.

Your compensation as a full-time employee generally includes subsidized health and dental insurance and a 401(k) match, which together can be worth many thousands of dollars. Paid sick days, vacation time, and holidays make your life easier and more enjoyable. Christmas bonuses are still the norm at some companies. Tech workers in particular may be offered restricted stock, stock options, or stock appreciation rights to entice them to stay at one company long-term.

Stock options and restricted stock

Restricted stock comes in several forms. Restricted stock awards give you stock in the company immediately, but it cannot be sold until after a certain period of time, when it vests. For an early stage startup where the stock value is low, the cost to purchase the shares or the taxes on shares provided as compensation will likewise be low. Additionally, as soon as you acquire them you start the holding period required to treat appreciation as long term capital gains.

Restricted stock units (RSUs) are essentially promises to give you shares of the company's stock after a certain period of time; they are worthless until they vest, after which you own stock in the company and they're worth money according to the company's share price. At vesting, if they are given as compensation, you'll owe taxes on the current value.

A stock option gives you the right to purchase a set number of shares in a company at a set price, determined when the option is issued; this is the grant (also called the exercise or strike) price. If the value of the stock increases, you can exercise the option to purchase shares at the cheaper strike price, which you then have the option of selling at the higher current price. Stock appreciation rights are similar, but rather than actually purchasing the stock, you simply receive the difference between the grant price and the current price.

Chapter Eight

Owning a business

Computer skills make it much easier to create a successful business, for multiple reasons.

1. Low barrier to entry. Starting any business requires a certain amount of time, effort, and money, but those involving coding may only require a computer, an internet connection, a good idea, and the skills to put the idea into practice. If you're reading this, chances are you already have most if not all of those. In some ways, this low barrier to entry is a disadvantage – it means more competition – but the upside is that you can attempt something with low risk[1] . To avoid investing too much time into something that might not be viable, you can put in just enough work to create something that people are likely to find useful and see if you can get paying customers before you invest in something more full-featured. This is called created a minimum viable product, or MVP.

2. Scalability. Someone with plumbing or mechanical skills may be

---

1. Daniel Vassallo refers to this as small bets – making a low-cost investment rather than going all-in on one big project.

able to build an excellent business, but because it depends directly on that person's time, it's difficult to scale. Someone with technical or writing skills can create something that can be used by many people, which removes that limitation[2].

3. Removal of geographical limitations. This is related to scaling, but rather than talking about reaching more people, we're talking about reaching the right people. If you create a very specialized tool that is only useful to a small subset of people, but is extremely useful to that group, you can do very well with that small but specialized audience[3]. To take a writing example, there are tools that are used by authors to help us find the keywords our target audience is using to search Amazon, so that we can properly target our advertising and get our books in front of the people who want them. These are tools with a very specific audience (mostly, self-published authors who sell on Amazon and are serious about

---

2. At the time of writing, one of my books has sold around 9,000 copies. That's 9,000 people potentially impacted by what I do. It would be very difficult for me to help that many people in person, especially in only three years.

3. This is called niching down – making content that is only relevant to a very specific audience.

4. Notice that this is exactly what I'm doing with this book – I'm writing something that's less useful to a general audience, but more useful to my target audience, which is people who have technical skills and don't have time for a lot of fluff. While I'm not charging a premium price, I expect this book to sell better than a generic personal finance book would because I'm (hopefully) providing my audience with exactly what they need.

writing as a business) that sell well to that audience. You don't have to niche down to be successful – I'm currently playing with an idea for a productivity app that will hopefully have wide appeal if I end up moving forward with it – but when you do, it lets you find a loyal audience (and charge more) because you are providing them with exactly what they need, rather than offering a general solution that works for more people but not as well. Anytime you can use the internet to reach a very specific customer base and resolve their particular pain point better than a more general solution could, you have the opportunity to position yourself as having a premium (and thus more desirable) product[4].

Tax considerations for business owners

Small business owners without employees will generally file taxes as either a sole proprietorship or an S-corporation. The difference is how business income is treated for tax purposes.

As a sole proprietor, business profits are simply reported on your individual tax return; aside from needing to pay self-employment tax, there's not a lot of difference from being on salary. The advantage is that there's also not a lot of extra paperwork. With this type of business, there's no

---

4. Notice that this is exactly what I'm doing with this book – I'm writing something that's less useful to a general audience, but more useful to my target audience, which is people who have technical skills and don't have time for a lot of fluff. While I'm not charging a premium price, I expect this book to sell better than a generic personal finance book would because I'm (hopefully) providing my audience with exactly what they need.

distinction between the business and the owner; you simply file a Schedule C as part of your personal tax return and pay tax on any profits at your individual tax rate. An LLC, discussed in the next section, doesn't change your tax liability but does give you legal separation from the business to protect your assets.

Owning a corporation gives you more options. An S-corp is also known as a passthrough corporation, because business profits are simply passed through to your individual tax return without being subject to corporate taxes. When all of the profits are taken out this way, this is largely equivalent to the sole proprietorship. However, it's also possible to pay yourself a reasonable salary (the exact definition of reasonable is somewhat nebulous and will depend on exactly what service you're providing) and take the rest of the business profits as investment income, which may be taxed at a lower rate. Additionally, owning a corporation provides additional ways to defer taxation, such as creating a SEP-IRA retirement plan and redirecting a significant portion of the business profits into tax-deferred retirement plan contributions, allowing up to $61,000[5] per year to flow directly into investments, untaxed.

LLCs

It's common for a small business to be organized as an LLC, or limited liability corporation, which then elects to be taxed as an S-corporation. This, again, means some extra paperwork. If done correctly, the LLC restricts the

---

5. Contributions are limited to 25% of net earnings. This is an employer-funded plan – the business puts in up to $61k, you don't put in anything – and can be funded in addition to money that you put in to other retirement plans.

liability of each owner to only what they have invested in the corporation, which protects their personal assets, while the tax election reduces how much is due in taxes. Real estate investors will commonly have one LLC for each property, in order to shield each property from any lawsuits involving the others. There are some formalities that have to be observed to keep the protection of an LLC; otherwise, someone suing can "pierce the corporate veil" to place your personal assets at risk.

Insurance

Sad to say, we live in a sue-happy society, and lawsuits are often required simply to assign legal blame so that an insurance company will make good on its obligations. As you can imagine, even if you win, lawyers are expensive. I carry liability insurance on my business and umbrella insurance for myself, so that if I'm ever sued for anything the insurance company will be the one fighting the lawsuit rather than me personally.

Chapter Nine

Passive income and financial freedom

The problem with starting your own business is that you may simply trade a job working for somebody else's business with a job working for your own. That's not all bad – the potential financial upside is a lot higher, and you get to be your own boss. On the other hand, you have a lot more responsibility, potentially less ability to take time off, and your #1 employee can be rather irritating.

Ideally, we would like to be making passive income, which is income that keeps coming in whether or not we're working. The way to do this with a small business is to create an asset that keeps paying you whether or not you're working on it. This could be a traditional business where you create processes your employees can follow, eventually removing all of your own responsibilities until you put yourself out of a job, or it can be creating a digital product which again can be sold without your immediate involvement. Note that just being digital doesn't make it passive; programmers work hard!

There's some debate over what counts as passive income – after all, pretty much anything other than inheriting stock, money, or real estate requires some work on your part – but our definition will be that it is income that keeps coming in even if you stop working.

Getting all of your income from one source – generally, a job – is risky because if it goes away, it's hard to pay your bills. Having multiple streams of income means you're no longer totally reliant on any one of them, and having passive income streams makes it easier to keep that up. I feel like I was less stressed once my side hustle started consistently bringing in enough money to pay my mortgage, as we now had two independent sources of income sufficient to keep a roof over our heads.

Some people say that you should use your 9-5 (job) to pay the bills while you use your 5-9 (time) to build an asset that will replace the 9-5. Remember, though, that having an extra source of income doesn't mean you have to quit your job; it just means that you can survive without it. I suspect most programmers would go crazy without work to do; the goal is to be working because you want to, not because you have to.

Chapter Ten

Real estate

Owning rental property

The advantage of owning rental property is that someone else is paying your mortgage for you. Because you can purchase the asset while putting down 20% of the cost, with your renters eventually paying the other 80% while you reap 100% of the gain in value, owning rental real estate is one of the most popular and successful ways to generate wealth.

However, there are also a number of disadvantages:

- Higher interest rates for investment properties
- The risk that you aren't able to successfully rent the property
- The risk that the renter might damage the property or refuse to pay
- The need to either maintain the property yourself or pay a property management company to do so

In 2020, up to 10 percent of landlords with mortgages opted into forbearance and 7 percent missed mortgage payments due to lack of rent.

While owning rental property is generally profitable, it is neither hands-off nor risk-free.

Also, there are laws protecting renters that you must follow, particularly when screening potential tenants. To ensure you're following the laws, you'll need to work with a local real estate lawyer.

As we discussed in the section on taxes, real estate (both in terms of owning your own home and owning investment property) has many tax advantages, but that's not the only thing making it an attractive investment.

Buying real estate generally gives you access to something incredibly useful: OPM, or other people's money. **Using OPM gives you leverage**: your gains (and losses) are magnified because you are exposed to a larger amount of risk relative to the amount you are investing.

For example, suppose you purchase a $200k house and put the standard 20% ($40k) down, then rent it out for enough money to cover the mortgage, taxes, and other expenses. If the value of the house then increases to $240k, this is a 20% increase relative to the purchase price but a 100% increase relative to the amount of money you actually put down. An investor with $200k to spend, rather than purchasing one property, will use OPM to purchase five properties and reap the corresponding rewards.

Of course, this comes with corresponding risk as well; if the market drops 20%, the investor has now lost his entire down payment!

Owning and renting your home both come with their own advantages. Renting gives you more flexibility, as you're only tied to one place until the end of the lease; you also have fewer things that you're financially responsible for. Owning gives you more freedom to do what you want, and allows you to acquire equity. One of the primary considerations for which is better is how long you plan to stay in one place. As selling a home comes with considerable expenses, it's generally better to rent unless you plan to either stay in one place long term (more than three years) or rent out the property after you move out.

However, we also need to consider possible appreciation or depreciation. As long as we stay in a house we own, this may not make much difference other than adjustments to the property taxes. However, owning a home with a fixed rate mortgage means that even if property values (and thus rents) increase, our monthly payment (aside from taxes and insurance) is locked in, which gives us stability. At the time of this writing (late 2022), property values have increased significantly over the last few years, meaning that people who don't own property are now farther away from being able to purchase due to higher down payment requirements, while property owners who need to move at least have a (hopefully) appreciated property they can sell to fund the new property they wish to purchase.

Example

Consider a $500,000 home purchased with 20% down, with a 30-year mortgage at 3.25%, with annual property taxes of $8500 and homeowner's insurance of $1200. At the start of the loan, the monthly payment is $2550, of which $657 goes towards reducing the principle, $1083 goes towards interest, and the remainder goes to taxes and insurance. The immediate conclusion would be that this is a better value than renting if the cost of rent plus renter's insurance for an equivalent property is more than $1893 (the amount of the mortgage payment, minus the increased equity from paying down the principle). This neglects the cost of eventually selling the home, the possible tax deduction, and the cost of moving if the rental property becomes unavailable, but is a decent first approximation.

Buying a home

For most people, a home is by far the largest purchase they will ever make, and the process can be challenging. Particularly in a seller's market[1] , being prepared can make a huge difference in getting the home you want. A buyer who shows that they can close a deal quickly and with a minimum of hassle may find their offer accepted even if it wasn't the highest available[2] ; demonstrating that you can work within the seller's constraints without adding any of your own can be worth more than additional money.

The first step in home shopping (assuming you don't plan to pay cash) is to work with a lender to determine how much you're able to spend. This keeps you from wasting time pursuing houses that are (too far) out of your price range, while also keeping you from missing out on the perfect house because you don't have your pre-approval letter ready when it's time to submit an offer. The pre-approval letter confirms that the lender is willing to lend you a certain amount of money, which shows that you have the financial ability to move forward with a purchase. If the approval isn't for as much as you had expected, you can either change the range you're looking at or work to increase the amount of the approval, such as by paying down debt.

---

1. In a seller's market, the demand for homes exceeds the supply; homes tend to sell quickly and for high prices. See: 2021

2. When I purchased my home in 2021, I actually lost out on one house I bid on to someone with a lower bid, but who presumably didn't have contingencies.

2. When I purchased my home in 2021, I actually lost out on one house I bid on to someone with a lower bid, but who presumably didn't have contingencies.

Most buyers will benefit from working with a Realtor, a professional who helps with real estate transactions. A good Realtor will learn your preferences to help find homes that suit you, get you home tours at times that are convenient for you, point out issues with a home that you may have missed, and handle all the paperwork and negotiation. Realtors generally get new business through referrals, so it's to their advantage to make sure you're satisfied; you'll want to find someone who comes highly recommended and who you are personally comfortable with[3] . You want to avoid anyone who doesn't communicate well or promptly, doesn't seem honest or professional (for example, being late to your appointments or being unfamiliar with local housing regulations), or doesn't treat you as a priority even if you have a smaller budget.

Realtors are paid by the seller as a percentage of the sale price. Although both the buyer's and seller's Realtors are paid by the seller, they should be different people as the job of the listing agent is to represent the seller's interests, not yours.

Once you find a home to purchase, your offer will state the amount you're willing to pay, the amount of time the seller has to accept the offer, and any contingencies. Generally buyers want to get an answer as quickly as possible so they can win the property or move on, while sellers want to take their time in the hopes that a larger offer will come in. Once you've made the offer, you are legally committed to follow through until the time limit expires, the seller declines the offer, or you formally cancel the offer.

The most common contingencies in an offer are financing and inspections. A financing contingency means the sale goes through only if the

---

3. I and my immediate family have used the same Realtor to purchase four homes and sell one in the last decade. That's good repeat business!

lender approves your loan. This will be in almost all offers, but does give an advantage to cash buyers as there's no risk of the loan not being approved[4] . However, purchasing in cash means you don't get to take advantage of using OPM as described at the beginning of the Real Estate chapter. An inspection contingency means the buyer has the right to have a home inspector go through the house (at the buyer's expense) looking for issues and cancel the sale if any come up. The contingency will specify whether the seller has the right to keep the contract in place by fixing the issue.

Another common contingency is that the buyer's current house has to sell before closing. A contract contingency is common if the buyer currently has a home, as the proceeds from selling the old home are likely needed towards the down payment on the new home, but make your offer less attractive to sellers as it introduces additional risk of the sale not going through. This contingency can be avoided by getting approved for a bridge loan, which covers the cost of your down payment until your original home sells[5] .

---

4. My dad once thought he'd sold his house. Then the prospective buyer quit his job and bought a new car the week before closing. The loan, and the sale, did not go through.

4. My dad once thought he'd sold his house. Then the prospective buyer quit his job and bought a new car the week before closing. The loan, and the sale, did not go through.

5. After losing out on a few homes I bid on, I asked my lender for approval for one of these. My lender verified that I would qualify for one, then simply gave me a new pre-approval letter that no longer required that my old house close before the new one did. The next offer I put in didn't have the contract contingency and was accepted.

In some markets, where multiple offers may be involved, contracts may include an elevator clause, which automatically increases the offer up to a maximum if other, higher offers are received. The disadvantage of including one is that it shows the seller you're willing to pay more, which may make them less likely to accept your original offer.

Financing a home

When taking out a home loan, there are two factors under your control: the down payment and the length of the loan.

While there are many special programs that reduce the required down payment (particularly for first time homebuyers and veterans) you generally need at least 5% down to purchase a home and 20% down to avoid PMI. PMI, or private mortgage insurance, is insurance that you pay for to protect the lender if you default. It's expensive and you don't get anything for it, so I recommend avoiding it.

The most common mortgages are fixed-rate, 15- or 30-year loans. Fixed rate means that the interest rate is fixed; the loan payment may vary due to changes in property taxes and insurance rates, but the amount spent on paying down the loan (principle plus interest) will be consistent from month to month. A 15-year mortgage will have a lower interest rate than a 30-year mortgage; combined with higher monthly payments, the loan is paid off much faster and at much lower total cost. However, interest rates on a primary residence are generally low enough that a 30-year mortgage, with its lower monthly payment, makes the most financial sense for most peopl e[6].

With a fixed rate mortgage, you're locking in the same interest rate for many years. If rates drop, you can refinance and get a cheaper loan, but if they rise, you don't get hit by the higher rates. An adjustable rate mortgage, or ARM, doesn't have the long lock-in period; after a set time the rate will fluctuate. A 5/1 ARM, for example, will have the interest rate locked in for five years, after which it will be reset annually (the 1) to the current rate. The advantage of these loans is that because the lender isn't facing the risk that interest rates will rise dramatically while your rate stays low, the initial rate will be lower than for a fixed rate mortgage. As a result, these loans can be worthwhile for people who plan to own a property for only a few years [7] or who expect to be able to pay off the mortgage at the end of the fixed rate period.

Investing in real estate

---

6. Of course, finances aren't the only consideration. Some people will feel more comfortable having their home paid off as soon as possible, so it may make sense for them to go with a shorter mortgage. Also, interest rates have been much higher in the past – over 18% in the early 80s, during a period of extremely high inflation.

7. Keeping in mind that the expenses involved in selling a home mean that if you only live in the same place for a few years, renting will generally be cheaper than buying. The breakeven point tends to be at around five years, although this accounts for the increased equity from paying down the debt vs the costs of selling, and dramatic changes in housing costs can alter this calculation considerably.

Real estate has long been a popular income stream, but it comes with its own challenges. There are two main ways to invest in real estate. The easier method is to purchase a REIT, or Real Estate Investment Trust, which is a company that owns, operates, or finances income-producing properties and is generally traded like a stock. A REIT does have certain legal requirements, the most relevant of which is that it must pay at least 90% of its taxable income in the form of dividends. As a result, the REIT doesn't tend to appreciate much (but of course the dividends can be automatically reinvested). I like holding a REIT inside a retirement account, where the fact that the returns are taxed as regular income is irrelevant.

Actually owning your own rental property can be more lucrative, but also riskier, requires a larger investment, and involves more work. Purchasing an investment property generally requires at least 20% down, and the mortgage will have a higher interest rate than for an owner-occupied property[8]. Of course, it's possible to get around this by purchasing a duplex, triplex, or quadplex and living in one unit while renting out the others. In this case, it's also easier to respond to repair requests and collect rent checks since you're already right there.

One popular strategy for investors with children in college is to purchase a multiple-unit property for the child to live in[9]. The child is responsible for doing simple maintenance and collecting the rent checks, and the

---

8. If you've purchased a home recently, you may recall having to attest that you plan to live in it when signing the loan paperwork.

9. One way to do this is with a Shared Equity Financing Agreement or Shared Equity Mortgage, where the parent is the investing owner and the child is the occupying owner.

rented units make the mortgage payment more affordable than renting an apartment in a college town.

Depreciation

Depreciation is the process by which you write off a business purchase over time. This applies to business property which is used to produce income, is expected to last for more than a year, and has a determinable useful life.

Conceptually, this makes a lot of sense for something like a printer, which might have an average useful lifespan of so many years and thus the purchase price can be amortized over that lifespan.

Real estate doesn't generally get used up, but for taxes we pretend it does. Even while a property is gaining in value, the IRS assumes that it's actually losing value! As a result, you can write off this depreciation every year, essentially declaring a loss even while your investment property is making money. The land itself cannot be depreciated, but the buildings on the land can be depreciated over 27.5 years (for residential rental property). This means that each year that your property is in service as a rental, you can write off 3.636% of the building value.

The depreciation will be recaptured when you sell the property, but this can be indefinitely delayed by doing a 1031 exchange, which allows you to roll the proceeds from a sale into another investment property (thus restarting the depreciation timer) and defer paying capital gains[10] tax until you sell that property as well. (Of course, tax liability ends with death, so if you still own the property when you die, it can pass to your heirs at

10. Capital gains tax is what you pay on long-term investments that increase in value.

its stepped-up market value, avoiding the capital gains and depreciation recapture).

Chapter Eleven

Retirement

What does retirement mean to you?

Some people dream of moving to Florida and playing golf every day. Others want to travel the world. Still others are happy to just keep working part-time and walking to the park in the afternoon.

Retirement is the point in your life when you no longer work (although many people semi-retire, working part time or when they feel like it). Our goal is to reach the point where we do not need to work, because we have sufficient savings or passive income to meet our financial needs.

One frequent error that people make when calculating how much money they'll need is to base it on their income while working. This is the wrong metric, because both your spending and saving will change once you're retired. On the spending side, you no longer have the expenses associated with your previous job, but you may wish to take up new and expensive hobbies. Additionally, if you're not over 65 (and thus eligible for Medicare), you'll need to account for health insurance. On the savings side, you're now drawing from your retirement account rather than contributing to it, so you only have to replace the portion of your income that was actually going to expenses. Additionally, depending on what kind of income you have, it may be (partially or entirely) nontaxable.

It's wise to take a mini-retirement before it's time for the real thing, so you can see how you handle no longer going in to work. Maybe you'll love it, or maybe you'll go stir-crazy after a few weeks and desperately need to find something to do. These are good things to know before you're permanently out of work!

Once you have an idea of how much your living expenses will be in retirement, you can calculate how much you'll need. Your income could (and hopefully, will) come from a variety of sources.

If you're 62 or older, you have the option of taking Social Security (although it will be a permanently reduced amount if you're younger than your full retirement age, which will be between 65 and 67 depending on when you were born). You can check your benefit amount by logging in at ssa.gov. Up to 85% of your benefit will be taxable.

Subtract your monthly Social Security benefit and any passive income you have from your monthly needs; this is the amount you'll need to withdraw each month from your retirement savings. On average, the stock market returns about 7% per year, adjusted for inflation. A useful rule of thumb is that withdrawing no more than 4% of your account each year will allow the account to keep growing over time. This means that the account will need to be at least 25 times the amount you will withdraw annually.

If you have both traditional and Roth accounts, some of the money you withdraw may be nontaxable. You may choose to withdraw enough money from your traditional account to bring you to the top of one tax bracket, then withdraw enough from the Roth account to meet your remaining needs.

The above calculation assumes that you want your retirement account to continue to grow indefinitely. Another approach is to assume a fixed lifespan and allow the account to shrink so long as it does not reach zero before you reach the age by which you expect to pass away. For myself, I prefer to assume that I'll live forever – or if not, at least I'll have a decent nest egg to pass on to my children.

Chapter Twelve

Estate planning

It's a subject that's not always pleasant to think about: what happens when we're no longer around?

If nobody depends on you, this might not be something you need to worry about. But if you have a family and expect to leave behind an estate, it's worth taking the time to make sure that the people you care about will be taken care of after your death. This means leaving behind documents with the following information:

- What should happen to your possessions? If you don't leave behind a will, then the laws in your state will determine who gets what, which may not be what you intended.
- If you have ongoing obligations, who will take over for you?
- What bank accounts and insurance policies do you have?
- What are the logins and passwords for your accounts?
- Who needs to be notified of your death?

Thy will be done

A will lays out your wishes for the disposition of your assets and the care of your dependents. You can have one prepared for you by an attorney who specializes in estates, or you can create one yourself or use will-creation software. If creating one yourself, it's important to sign it in the presence of witnesses (who will also sign) to make it harder to challenge. The presence of witnesses provides proof that you actually wrote and signed the will. Preferably, have disinterested witnesses – someone who is not a beneficiary.

Generally speaking, if you are married then your spouse is entitled to a minimum percentage of your estate, as specified by state law; otherwise, you may dispose of your property as you see fit. Specifically disinheriting a family member (generally an adult child) in your will indicates that you no longer view them as your heir and thus doesn't leave open the possibility that you simply forgot to list them (which could be considered grounds to challenge the will, with a court possibly awarding equal shares to children not named). If you do not have a spouse or children, then your estate by default will pass to your closest relatives, unless you specify otherwise.

Many of your assets can be transferred simply by naming beneficiaries. Examples include retirement plans and insurance policies; you can specify who they should pay in the event of your death. As long as they don't pay to your estate, they won't be included in the assets to be divided up.

Trusts and avoiding probate

While a will is the first step in estate planning, it may still have to go through probate, which is the process of settling your affairs after death. Assets that have a beneficiary designated, as discussed above, can pass directly to that person, while jointly owned assets will pass to the surviving owner. If no will is found or for large estates, the remaining assets may go through the probate process, which can take months or years to complete. This can be avoided by limiting the number of assets you have that are subject to probate.

A trust is a legal entity which is set up to hold assets. It is managed by a trustee who has a fiduciary duty to manage it in the best interests of the trust's beneficiaries. A living trust allows you to avoid probate because the assets being passed on have been transferred to the trust and are no longer part of your estate. The trust is commonly set up as revocable, with the owner (you) as trustee, which means that you maintain full control over the assets until your death or incapacity.

Settling your debts

As a general rule, nobody else is responsible for your debts. If you don't intend to leave an estate to anyone, then you don't have to plan for how your debts will be paid off after your death. The exception is if someone else was already jointly responsible for your debt, such as if you had a co-signer on a loan. It's not unheard of for debt collection agencies to harass survivors to pay off your debts, even if there are no legal obligations, so even if you don't expect to leave an estate this is something to be aware of.

Passwords and other access

If you do plan to leave an estate, particularly if that includes assets such as cryptocurrencies that may only exist in a digital wallet, be sure you have a document that will let your survivors access those assets – and that they know about it! This doesn't need to be an official document, just something that lists all of your accounts and how to get to them.

Taxes

For most people, the federal estate tax (sometimes called the death tax) isn't worth worrying about, as the first $12.92 million of your estate is exempt. Assets being transferred to your surviving spouse aren't subject to the tax, nor are those contained in an irrevocable trust.

Chapter Thirteen

Insurance

Insurance: the product we buy hoping not to use it. How much do you actually need?

Renter's insurance

If you rent, renter's insurance covers the cost of replacing your possessions if something happens to them. The landlord's insurance covers his property, not yours; if the house burns down and you're uninsured, you're probably on your own.

Homeowner's insurance

Homeowner's insurance covers both the home being insured and the owner's personal property. To protect their investment, banks will generally require that you hold a large enough policy to pay off the mortgage if something happens to the house. The policy may cover replacement cost rather than actual value, if for some reason it would cost more to rebuild the property than it's worth. Personal property doesn't have to actually be in the home when something happens for it to be covered, and riders are available to cover particularly valuable property (such as artwork, cameras, and jewelry).

Flood insurance

Homeowner's insurance does not cover damage caused by flooding, where a flood involves water damaging multiple properties. Unlike homeowner's insurance, this is optional. It's also expensive, so many people choose to forgo it. Just be aware that a flood can render your home uninhabitable, and your regular insurance won't cover it.

Health insurance

Medical costs are the #1 cause of bankruptcy in America. If you don't have medical insurance, get it.

If you're over 65, this is probably going to be Medicare. Under 65, if you're employed full time, you'll likely get the best rate going through your employer. Otherwise, search for a policy at healthcare.gov.

In the past, many people in need of care were dismayed to find that the insurance they thought they had was actually a junk policy that didn't cover much, but the Affordable Care Act of 2010 put in place minimum standards for coverage. Variables you'll want to pay attention to are the premiums (how much do you pay each month?), the network (which doctors can you see?), co-pays and deductibles (how much do you have to pay per visit?), and out of pocket maximums (how much can you owe per year, on top of your premiums?).

Dental insurance

The mouth, apparently, is not part of the body, and as such must be insured separately. Dental insurance tends to be much less comprehensive than medical insurance; it covers routine preventative care and a limited amount of additional care, after which you're on the hook for the rest. Find a good dentist in your area and get what they accept.

Disability insurance

If you were in an accident and were unable to work for several months or even years, would you be able to pay your bills? Long- and short-term disability insurance pays a percentage of your salary if you're unable to return to work after a given period of time (generally one to two weeks). I carry both. I knew someone who gave his up to save money, which he regretted when he was forced to stop working due to cancer. This will cost hundreds of dollars a year, but for someone with a highly compensated job, I think it's worth it.

Life insurance

Do you have people who would struggle if you weren't around, because they rely on either your income or your labor[1] ? If so, then you need life insurance. If you're single with no dependents, you probably don't.

I like to carry enough insurance to pay off all of my family's debts (including our house if needed), with enough left over for my wife and kids to live on for several years. It's relatively cheap peace of mind to know that if something happens to me, my family is taken care of.

---

1. Stay at home parents may not earn money, but they still provide a valuable service that would be expensive to replace!

Auto insurance

Just listed for completeness. If you drive, you have to have it. I generally prefer a policy with larger deductibles in exchange for smaller premiums.

Umbrella insurance

If all of the above wasn't enough, umbrella insurance covers you if you get sued and your other insurance isn't sufficient to cover it. It will require already having other insurance policies that meet minimum standards. I like this for someone who does something that could potentially open them up to liability[2].

---

2. My original motivation for getting an umbrella policy was that I was a foster parent at the time and I wanted to be covered in case any of my kids did anything that I could be found liable for. Having a business seemed like sufficient reason to keep it. We live in a sue-happy society and I'd rather my insurance company have a vested interest in defending me from any lawsuits.

Chapter Fourteen

Conclusion

Each of the chapters in this book could be a book on its own (and indeed, I've read dozens of books on these topics). Finance is a fascinating topic, but the preceding chapters have covered what you need to know to be able to manage your own financial wellbeing.

While I hope you found this book interesting, what I really want is for you to take action. This could be as simple as increasing your 401(k) contribution to max out the matching funds or as complex as starting your own business. There's no better time to take control of your financial future.

Key takeaways:

- Avoid bad debt
- Get the maximum 401(k) match
- When your income is low, invest in a ROTH
- Avoid lifestyle inflation
- If you plan to work for yourself, understand how much money you actually need

- Before starting a business, ask yourself what pain point you're resolving for your customers
- To maximize the upside of a business, be sure it can scale
- Where possible, take advantage of OPM (other people's money)

Made in the USA
Monee, IL
04 November 2026

67375589R00036